HOW TO

START YOUR OWN

APPRENTICESHIP

PROGRAM

Written from a Construction Perspective

JESSICA LEWIS

MOBU ENTERPRISES

Developmental editing by Johnnie Mazzocco
Other editing and design by Indigo: Editing, Design, and More
- Line editing: Ali Shaw
- Proofreading: Sarah Currin and Kristen Hall-Geisler
- Cover design, interior layout, and ebook conversion: Vinnie Kinsella

ISBN: 978-0-578-74063-8
eISBN: 978-0-578-74064-5

This book is dedicated to my grandmother Annie Robinson and my aunts Laura Sabador, Ann Minor, Eleanor Robinson, Estelle Izzard, Darcel Lackey, Rho Izzard, and Evelyn Morris, the matriarchs in my family who always supported me through all my risky business and personal endeavors without judgment and with full confidence in my capabilities. I am thankful for all you have done to encourage and foster my creativity and self-esteem. I would like to also thank a few awesome book readers, who gave me great insight on how the book made them feel. Thank you Xavier Lee, Anna Robinson, Prudence Ojurongbe, Jamarr Jones, Bee Daniels, and Aisha Thompson.

Contents

Preface

I started this journey in the construction field ten years ago as a consultant and worked as a project manager and an operations manager before becoming a chief executive officer when I launched my own construction firm in 2018. I've specialized in everything from project management to lead design and have seen some amazing transformations in homes, business buildings, and properties over the years.

What I enjoyed the most as a project manager was being able to teach others how to prioritize, organize, and channel their energy in a constructive way to save money and time when completing small- and large-scale projects. I also enjoyed watching some of my family members develop land and rehab houses. It was an indescribable joy, like being a proud parent looking on as your baby walks for the first time, or like painting your best artwork and sharing it with the world. It's a fantastic experience to see your hard work come to life. In construction, this is especially true if you enjoy problem-solving and being a visionary.

After two years owning my own construction firm, I became interested in launching an apprenticeship program to help others gain experience with the ins and outs of the industry. But this is easier said than done—just as certifications are required to do construction or other professional work, an apprenticeship program must be approved, and it's a good idea to consider registering it too. Registering an apprenticeship program with the Department of Labor (DOL) is perfect for any employer who desires technical assistance to ensure their program runs smoothly.

I embarked on the journey of registering my apprenticeship program, but sheesh, this was like trying to open a locked box with the instructions on the inside. Yes, I know that does not make sense—that's exactly how I felt too. I found that going through this process would have been easier if there were step-by-step instructions on exactly what to do and what to expect. When I finally successfully navigated the process and launched my company's program, I decided to write this book to guide others through the process as well. My experience is in construction, so this comes from a construction perspective, but most of the information can be applied to any industry.

The most important information you will receive is how to identify your program needs and outline them effectively. Doing so will make it easier for you to communicate that to your education partner and create a program that is mutually beneficial for you, your apprentices, and your education partner. It is also important to identify your target audience; this will help you identify the areas of instruction you want to focus on.

This book is ideal for anyone who wishes they could duplicate themselves. Maybe you're a sole operator and are scrambling to keep up with demand, or maybe there is a shortage of highly skilled workers in your industry. Either way, an apprenticeship program can help you train superior workers, and this book illustrates a simple yet comprehensive curriculum for that purpose. This book is also for any business owner who still works in their business and wants to get out of the rat race. A mark of a successful business is when you as the owner get to step *out* of the business to do the things you enjoy because you have competent team members who won't burn the building down as soon as you leave. A registered apprenticeship program will help you achieve that dynamic.

I hope this book will give you a sense of structure behind the creation of an apprenticeship program along with practical steps for how to pull all the pieces together. I find it helpful when someone shows me the whole picture because I learn visually and experientially. This book will have written steps, corresponding video on my website, examples, and resources to help paint that picture. With these resources and your own dedication, I feel confident you can launch your program within thirty days.

Cheers to your success. Feel free to request consultations or give me feedback at shippingliving@gmail.com—that's my private email box.

—Jessica Lewis
June 2020

Introduction

Before we get into the specifics of *how* to set up a registered apprenticeship program, it's best to examine *why* you should do so and *what* exactly it means to set up an apprenticeship program. Let's start with these foundational questions and answers:

What is an apprenticeship? An apprenticeship is a program designed to teach skills in any industry to a potential permanent employee, while that employee is being paid, for a period not less than two years. Typically, the program includes specific curriculums related to that industry along with on-the-job training designed to connect the in-class learning to practical skills.

What is a pre-apprenticeship? A pre-apprenticeship is a requirement that must be completed before the apprenticeship begins. In the case of construction or any trade-related programs, a pre-apprenticeship would teach the basics of that trade (for example, an Introduction to Plumbing class). It functions to help the participant identify which track they will pursue, solidify commitment from the participant, and prepare them to go full force into the next phase: the apprenticeship.

Both apprenticeships and pre-apprenticeships are much like work-study or internship programs in college or Job Corps. These programs basically pay participants to study and work at the same time, earn a diploma or certificate, and receive scaled wages as they complete milestones. Apprenticeships are excellent in comparison to work-study programs and internships because participants are guaranteed a career upon completion. Imagine being paid to go to school, earning a diploma, and securing a guaranteed job. As for the employer, you trained them up to be ideal employees, so you know their competencies and areas of opportunity, all of which you can play a part in improving.

How can it benefit you? Creating an apprenticeship will help you build a superior workforce. I would say we as business owners desire three important things: One, to have competent employees. Two, to have an organizational culture that breeds productivity and growth of business. Three, to make money. Let's be honest—some people want money more than the other two goals, but focusing on the other two, if done correctly, will bring the money. This is where the apprenticeship program comes in to save the day and your business. By training competent employees, you will create a high-performing organizational culture, and that in turn will affect your bottom line in a great way! Competently trained people + high-performing culture = $$$$. This formula is for any business type. In construction, poorly trained workers can lead to injuries and death, so emphasizing training and competence is critical. This is the catalyst behind creating a strong program.

How will it benefit the participant? Any participant who decides to join your program will be able to earn while they work. Some can receive financial assistance to attend local schools, much of it in the form of grants, saving them money over time. The ultimate benefit is the certification and the permanent employment they will earn upon completion. Completing an apprenticeship does take a commitment of at least two years, but if they are looking for a career rather than a job, then this is a perfect opportunity for them. Nothing beats guaranteed money.

Who can help make the apprenticeship a success? You, the participant, and your partners will all drive the progress of the program and help each other to be successful. By providing the platform, finding industry education partners, and creating a permanent job for the participant, you will help the economic landscape in your city, improve the participant's way of life, and drive your business to the top.

What's the difference between registered and unregistered apprenticeships? To be or not to be registered, that is the question. Well, it comes down to preference. Being registered allows for the entire country to know you exist and gives you a lot of indirect exposure because you will be on the federal database for apprenticeships where other employers, education partners, and participants will see your business. Furthermore, depending on your target applicant demographics, there can be monetary benefits to being registered because programs like the Workforce Innovation Opportunity Act (WIOA) can pay your participants for taking part in your registered apprenticeship program. Unregistered programs will still get tax breaks for hiring certain populations (such as ex-offenders), and both, if done correctly, could receive referrals from technical schools for students to complete on-the-job training so you don't have to go looking for applicants. That said, the official registered database is often the first place people look and is searchable by industry and location, so it's much easier for people to find your program.

I chose for my apprenticeship program to be registered, and the rest of the book will illustrate how exactly my company navigated the labyrinth of the Registered Apprenticeship Program and the steps that you can follow to get through the maze with ease.

Keep in mind that the DOL core elements for registered apprenticeship programs include a paying job, on-the-job learning, in-class learning, a 1:1 mentor-to-student ratio, and earned credentials. There are also other categorizations to consider, such as employer-sponsored, educator-sponsored, and intermediary-sponsored programs. An employer-sponsored program allows full autonomy on how the program is created and run. An educator-sponsored program divides the control between the educator and the employer. Lastly, an intermediary-sponsored program is a combination of the two. All three will receive technical assistance from the DOL. The DOL has a host of information about all of this on its website, listed in the Further Resources section at the back of the book.

Can I set up an apprenticeship program in my industry? The process explained in this book for setting up an apprenticeship programs, can be used for any industry that has a need for a superior workforce. It can be in finance, culinary, or even retail, to name a few examples. The key to a successful workforce is training. An apprenticeship (registered or unregistered) is designed to offer in-class training and mentoring that leads to a certification and an increase in income or job responsibility. My industry is construction, but there are over 1,400 occupations available for apprentices. Your DOL representative (rep) can assist you in fine-tuning an apprenticeship program in your industry so it will meet your needs. And guess what—maybe yours will be the first of its kind and you can set the framework for future companies in your industry. If you are not sure, ask.

What challenges will I face in this process? Everyone's journey is unique, but I can tell you that most people face *some* sort of challenge in launching an endeavor of this size. Some of the ones you might come across—as well as my suggestions for how to solve them—include the following:

- DOL apprenticeship website inoperable: Use the help link at the top of the page.
- DOL rep cannot be identified or reached: Use the help link.

- Errors on the submission of your application: Use the help link.
- Having a hard time finding schools that have in-class sessions: Ask for help from your DOL rep. Google technical schools near you.
- Trouble finding community partners: Google non-profits or for-profits in your industry. It may also be helpful to maybe go back to the schools you attended, associations you belong to, or other organizations you may be a part of to ask if they would want to partner. Lastly, some of my program's partners have branches in other cities; search for the name in my partner list, and then swap out your state or city.
- Difficulty making your outline: Google "Course outline for _____," filling in the blank with the type of program.
- No in-class curriculums available in your area: If you are not able to find an in-class curriculum, you can still have a training program—it just cannot be registered with the DOL. This commonly occurs when no formal training exists for your industry. An example may be mold remediation.
- Can't find apprentices: Contact your local DOL branch. Contact local schools (high schools and adult technical schools).
- Can't find instructors: Contact your local DOL branch for help. Post a job opening.
- Not sure how many hours are needed in the program: The DOL application will help you, but if for some reason you cannot find your occupation, message your DOL office.

Can you help me set up my program? I'm happy to help! I provide consulting services through Real Solutions for

Real People. Please see www.rs4rp.com for more information on services and consulting rates.

In the rest of this book, we'll look at the specifics of how to set up your apprenticeship program and apply to register it. There are four parts to the book, which I've named according to the courses of a satisfying meal: Part I is the snacketizer, a small bit of information to give you a taste of the full process. Part II, the appetizer, expands on that a little more. Part III is the meat and potatoes—the heart of the event. Part IV is the dessert, meaning what you get to enjoy after the program is set up, registered, and running. Reading *How to Start Your Own Apprenticeship Program: Written from a Construction Perspective* will give you the full meal.

PART I

The Snacketizer

CHAPTER 1

What You Need to Know

A s with any new business endeavor, before you can begin, you've got to get a clear vision of your idea. What do you want it to accomplish? Who do you envision participating? What resources will you use to make it a reality? Beyond that, though, apprenticeships have specific requirements that must be factored in. Use these categories to help you brainstorm your idea and home in on your apprenticeship vision.

Apprenticeship Program Requirements

Mentors Who Will Do the On-the-Job Training

Federal regulations require mentor-student ratios to be 1:1 for apprenticeship programs. If your program will be registered with the DOL, it is required that each participant has a mentor who can monitor, teach, and evaluate their learned competencies in the classroom and on the job.

I suggest you outline the curriculum your program will teach participants first. Then, next to each topic, list the names of a few veterans in your industry who are able and willing to teach the topics and give one-on-one mentoring. If your industry requires licensing, I would not recommend inviting unlicensed individuals to be your apprenticeship instructors. I know many people who learned their trades by doing, but this does not replace learning core competencies that are necessary to be successful in your industry. I call these people the bootleggers of the world—they have no formal training, but they "know" how to do certain tasks—though often this knowledge is incomplete or haphazard. Having a licensed individual will ensure shortcuts are not taken and the participants are gaining hands-on experience in conjunction with the book knowledge they are acquiring in their in-class training.

A Partnership with a Local Technical School

In construction, it's critical to attend trade school where you learn book knowledge so you can competently work in the industry with minimal mistakes, because those mistakes can mean injury or death. This is true for your apprenticeship participants, too. I'm sure you've heard enough about workplace accidents, so I will spare you the graphic descriptions, but however you gained your book knowledge in your respective industry, it would benefit you to expose your apprentices to the same process. You may have gone to a technical college, a specialty school for restaurant and hospitality management, or an online certification program from IBM, to name just a few examples. Whatever school you attended, partner with that school or one like it near you to help you design a curriculum that will be in alignment with the jobs you have available at your company and address the workplace challenges you may be experiencing.

The school you choose most likely will have classes that offer coursework similar to your position skill sets, and you should work with the school to create a partnership that makes sense for your company. For me, I wanted my participants to go straight from my curriculum to taking and passing the general contractor state exam without having to study fourteen books first. Code is different in certain states, but the technical school will teach the foundational principles, and then all the student has to add to their learning is the information specific to state codes. I chose Central Georgia Technical College as a regional school to partner with as well as Penn Foster, which is a national online school.

You can also partner with any youth trade school at the high school level. This route is not much different, except you would be working with Career Academy, Job Corps, or equivalent institutions that typically serve people between the ages of sixteen to twenty-three. All apprenticeship participants have to be age sixteen and up. In our case, we partnered with William S. Hutchings College and Career Academy in Macon, Georgia, because it offered construction management and other specialties to high schools across Bibb County, Georgia; we then expanded to other educational partners as we moved to different counties and states across the nation. Our apprentices went to their regular high school and attended Hutchings, and many were dually enrolled with Central Georgia Technical College as well.

Partnerships with Organizations That Match Your Target Audience or Industry (i.e., Trade Unions)

Community organizations that serve the demographics you want to see in your apprenticeship program can help you reach your target audience. Brainstorming and working with these organizations was the most fun for me. They have been pivotal to my execution because I wanted to work with ex-offenders, adults and young adults, and veterans in Georgia. Here is a list of my community partners and how they have helped me execute my apprenticeship program:

- A.D.A. Supplies, Inc.,[1] helps with purchasing the containers we use for construction projects.

---

1. https://adasupply.com/

- Central Georgia Technical College[2] is an education and curriculum partner for the State of Georgia.
- Department of Labor[3] is an apprenticeship partner and provides resources for both program creators and participants.
- Enviro Building Systems[4] is a SmartSteel manufacturer and a vendor we use for internal materials in our construction projects.
- GCubed, Inc.,[5] provides consulting for insight on the use of apprenticeships across varying industries.
- Georgia Correctional Industries[6] connects state inmates with hands-on learning opportunities through employment.
- Georgia Department of Community Supervision[7] helps me reach my target population of ex-offenders post-release.
- Georgia Department of Corrections[8] helps me reach my target population of ex-offenders pre-release.
- Georgia Vectr Center[9] helps me reach my target population of veterans in need of employment and has also been a business training partner.
- Green Hawk Solutions, LLC,[10] provides instruction for the apprentices and is also a co-owner of Mobu Enterprises (Mobu).

2. https://centalgatech.edu/academics/registered-apprenticeship
3. http://www.apprenticeship.gov/
4. https://envirobuildingsystems.com/
5. http://www.gcubedgroup.com/
6. http://gci-ga.com/
7. https://dcs.ga.gov/
8. http://dcor.state.ga.us/
9. https://gavectr.org/
10. https://facebook.com/green-hawk-solutions-llc/103400151093305

- HomePort Veterans Transition Home[11] provides a worksite for on-the-job training.
- The Macon-Bibb County Office of Small Business Affairs,[12] Economic and Community Development Committee,[13] Mayor's Office,[14] and Board of Commissioners[15] provide technical assistance in applying the apprenticeship program to local economic development.
- Macon Re-Entry Coalition[16] serves as a resource for community needs for employment.
- New Vision MSK[17] is a STEM program for young girls whose mission is increasing women in STEM fields.
- Operation HOPE, Inc.,[18] is an education and curriculum partner.
- Penn Foster[19] is an education and curriculum partner.
- Real Solutions for Real People[20] is an entrepreneur school curriculum creator and also provides consulting and business management instruction.
- SCORE[21] has been a business training partner.
- Technical College System of Georgia[22] is an education and curriculum partner.

---

11. https://homeportmaconga.org/
12. https://maconbibb.us/small-business-affairs
13. https://www.maconbibb.us/economic-community-development/
14. https://www.maconbibb.us/mayor/
15. https://maconbibb.us/commissioners
16. https://maconreentry.org/
17. http://www.newvisionmsk.org/
18. https://operationhope.org/
19. https://pennfoster.edu/career-school
20. https://rs4rp.com/
21. https://score.org/
22. https://tcsg.edu/

- United Way of Central Georgia[23] helps me reach my target population of veterans in need of training and employment.
- William S. Hutchings College and Career Academy[24] has been an education partner and also helps me reach my target population of youth in trade.

Note that unions can also be partners, but many union members are already working in the industry and may be licensed already, and thus your program may not fill a need for them. Additionally, many unions already have apprenticeship programs, so it may not benefit them specifically to partner with you. Quite naturally, they want to keep their own skilled workforce to themselves. But in the case where there is no conflict, contacting unions in your industry would help you get the word out about your program quicker. The union most likely already has a database of people who need the skill sets you offer in your program. Otherwise, focus on recruiting directly from trade schools and high schools, because they will connect you with participants as a reciprocal relationship.

23. https://unitedwaycg.org/
24. https://hutchings.bcsdk12.net/

PART II

The Appetizer

CHAPTER 2

Pre-Steps

Before you even begin, brainstorm the benefits of starting an apprenticeship program. If there are not more pros than cons, it may not be worth the adventure. You must also determine if you are willing to fully commit to this process because you may find yourself doing the implementation and mentorship alone initially or after you think you're finished—or even after the program is up and running. Furthermore, registered programs have a lot of requirements. In my opinion, the benefits are great for the strong-minded business owner who is willing to endure all the steps to complete the process, but it's not a journey to start on a whim. For more guidance, check out the DOL apprenticeship website listed in the Further Resources section at the back of the book.

Here is my list of pros and cons as I was considering starting Mobu's apprenticeship program:

Pros

- Job creation
- Support for local economy
- Free education for participant
- Grants and other funding opportunities
- Participant-led projects
- Help for underserved populations
- Improved business processes
- Future joint ventures and subcontracting opportunities
- Higher employee retention

- Creation of custom skill sets
- Increased productivity
- Steady supply of trained laborers
- Diverse workforce
- Lower recruitment costs
- Advancement opportunities

Cons

- Limits options for participants by locking them into the program for two years
- Long commitment for employer, mentors, and apprentices
- Higher company liability because people are likely to quit within the two-year period
- Potential burnout because apprentices might feel overworked before they are licensed or have completed school, and they may quit if they cannot balance school and work
- No guarantee for the company—participants could opt to go to school or work elsewhere

In sum, there are many pros as well as cons for all parties. Why a person chooses to participate is based on their long-term career objectives. Giving them the option to participate is a great start, showing them you care will create loyalty, and training them will help them to be competent employees.

CHAPTER 3

Choose a Name

We chose the Green Building Construction Apprenticeship Program offered by Mobu Enterprises for our name simply because it embeds our company's branding into the program and allows for us to *own* the name. When people do a search for our program in Google, it takes them directly to our social media profiles and our website, giving us free exposure. The more we are searched for, the more search engine optimization will eventually improve our rankings in search engines.

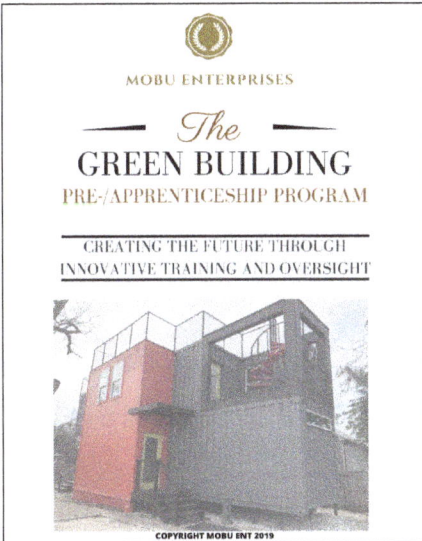

The Mobu Enterprises cover page matches our company's branding.

CHAPTER 4

Discuss Program Curriculum Topics

H ave a conversation with your team and discuss what will be taught and what participants will gain from joining the program. Here are the topics my team and I discussed and considered for our apprenticeship curriculum:

- Audit checklists
- Blueprint, site plan, and symbols literacy
- Building codes
- Building material usage
- Building material properties (UV durability, weatherability)
- Building site orientation
- Business etiquette 101
- CAD and basic mechanical drafting/illustration
- Construction standards
- Customer service and business organization
- Drainage, dry wells, and septic systems
- Drawing plans
- Effective communication on and off camera
- Effective online research
- Environmental regulations
- Foundation systems
- Green manufacturing materials and processes
- Greenhouse gases and buildings (ambient noise, radiant heat, hydronics)
- History of building science and methods

- Job hazard analysis
- Layout processes
- Leadership and critical thinking
- Marketing and selling your trade skills
- Math (geometry, arithmetic, trigonometry, algebra)
- Moisture migration and control
- Mold/indoor air quality and radon
- Occupational Safety and Health Administration (OSHA), Washington Industrial Safety and Health Act (WISHA), and industry safety procedures and regulations
- Principles of integrated design
- Recycling on site
- Specialty trade sequencing and scheduling
- Sustainability principles
- Technology-centered trade business
- Thermal and moisture protection
- Trade boss duties and responsibilities
- Vacant land strategic planning, purchasing, and development

Furthermore, what part will each person play in the execution of the plan? Although I launched our program mostly with some help and it turned out okay, it was difficult, and it can be frustrating if you have to figure out things on your own. Having a strong team will make this process much easier, and you will see positive results faster.

CHAPTER 5

Write Your Curriculum Outline

Depending on your industry, you will probably need to find coursework that aligns with your past experience as well as industry standards. To be registered with the DOL, you must use coursework from an accredited school. For example, we at Mobu are doing a construction apprenticeship, and we used curriculum topics from the National Center for Construction Education and Research and coordinated with our local technical school programs that are already in place. By making good use of existing coursework, you do not have to re-create the wheel and you can allow the resources to guide you.

But right now, you're just outlining and planning. This is preliminary and may change after you have a formal conversation with your local schooling systems. Write down all your ideas.

Our outline is here for your reference and review: Mobu Apprenticeship Outline.[25]

---

25. https://img1.wsimg.com/blobby/go/807062f6-4dee-4e85-98d2 -f243ff668a0b/downloads/AppendixA-WPS-RI-NonCBA-Final2020 .pdf?ver=1580265588478

<u>Competency-Based Occupation</u>: Please describe competencies required for the apprenticeship.

Work Process Schedule
Approximate Hours: 4,386

I. General Construction (866 hours)
II. Masonry (250 hours)
III. Carpentry (600 hours)
IV. Drywall (164 hours)
    a. Painting (137.50 hours)
V. Electrical (362.5 hours)
VI. HVAC (270 hours)
VII. Plumbing (290 hours)
VIII. Concrete (335 hours)
IX. Ironworks (345 hours)
X. Green Construction (440 hours)
XI. Project Management (234 hours)
XIII. Entrepreneur School (92 hours)

Mobu's apprenticeship program outline is easy to read at a glance.

CHAPTER 6

Search for Apprenticeships, Schools, and Representatives

Find out who your local technical school, career academies, and Department of Labor reps are. This allows you to view what similar apprenticeships already exist in your area to get a feel for what's already being offered as well as to consider how your program could be new and different. This can be Googled by simply searching for "technical schools" (or the relevant term) and your city name. You can also use the Apprenticeship Finder search on the DOL website, which yields both apprenticeships and technical schools, among other subjects.

I searched "Macon, Georgia," and "registered apprenticeships." I specifically wanted to know who else was running registered apprenticeship programs in Macon. This was first because I wanted to know who my competitors were and second, and more specifically, because I wanted to know who in my area had been willing to undergo this process in the hopes I could reach out to them. This search yielded zero results. I was lucky that there were no search hits for my industry; however, one result did come up when I added "construction" to the search terms, an unregistered program. What this meant was that I would be the only company marked in this industry and area as a registered program, lending me more credibility, exposure, and a heavy funnel for new participants. When you do this yourself, you may have to expand the geographic search area by changing the filters to get your local DOL rep or technical school. Just click on "Apply Filters" and change the radius.

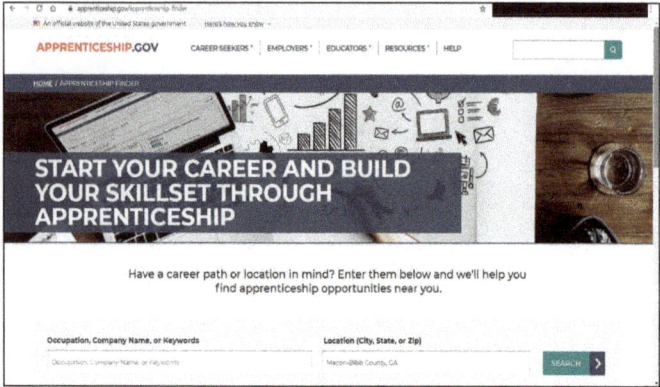

The Apprenticeship.gov search box will help you find apprenticeship programs in your area.

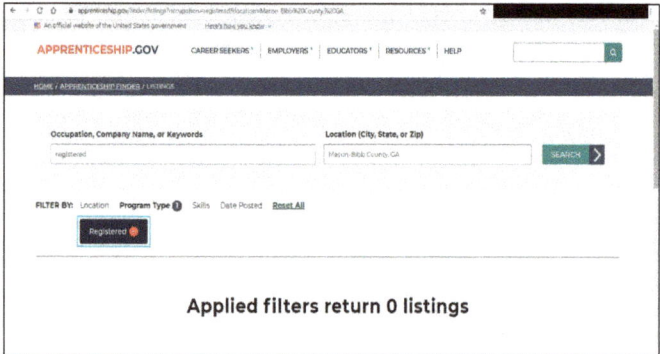

The Apprenticeship.gov filtered search will help you pinpoint resources specific to your needs.

After I received zero results for my initial search, I removed the filters, and over 1,700 apprenticeships came back. I was surprised that there were so many results, but I also realized I had to analyze the results to see what they were saying to me. Mainly, the results included apprenticeship programs, educators, and other resource partners, which was much more than I was looking for. Entering keywords helped find the results I needed. I would suggest keywords like "Department of Labor," "sponsor," or your geographic area. Eventually, you will get the results you desire.

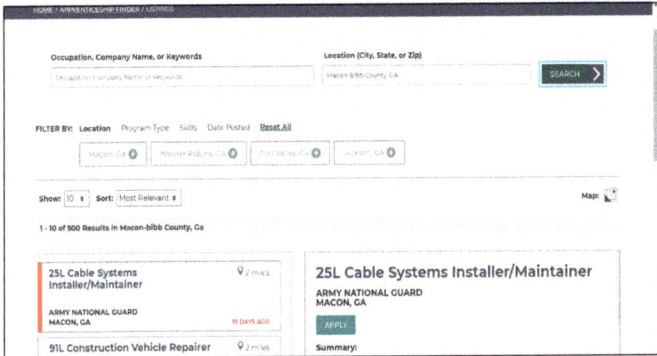

These search filters show results for apprenticeships near Macon, Georgia.

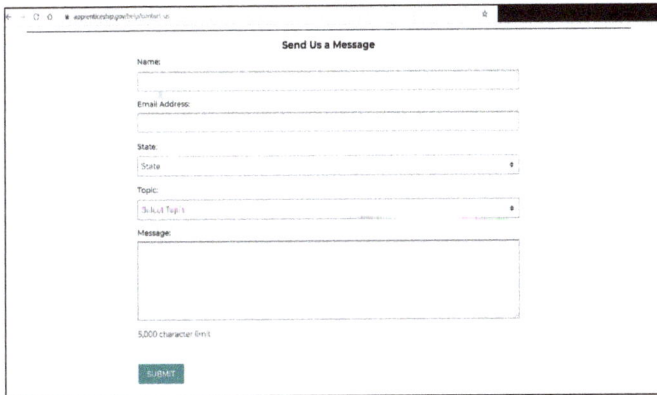

The Send Us a Message form looks like this when you click on the "Help" icon on the Apprenticeship.gov site.

If you are unable to find the results you need, send a message to the DOL help desk, and someone will get back to you. If you are anything like me, I had no idea what I was searching for (although I hope this book is helping you navigate the process easier). I ended up using the help desk contact form. At the bottom of the page on the left-hand side, under the DOL logo, there is a link that says "Contact Us." Don't be afraid to use it! HELP is also a topic header at the top of the main page.

CHAPTER 7

Research Education Partners

Choose which technical school best fits your plan for your apprenticeship program. Keep in mind that most programs will require at least 2,000 hours of apprenticeship work per year, some of which can be fulfilled through a combination of in-class experience and on-the-job training. Two factors that heavily influenced our choices were location and accessibility because we wanted our participants to have options between a local school that they could attend in person as well as a school that was available to them fully online if they chose. We selected Central Georgia Technical College and Penn Foster as our education partners because one is regional and the other is a national school, both offer similar coursework , and both were very helpful to me as I worked to create a program that aligned with my business model.

All students must apply for each school and adhere to the financial obligations of that institution. Some schools have financial aid, while others may not. The student will need to understand what is available, and that conversation will be between the school and the student. As an employer, this is not your responsibility. If you have an individual in mind, you can still hire them regardless of whether they apply and are accepted to school, or whether or not they receive financial aid. If they do not attend school, they just would be a standard employee and not part of your registered apprenticeship program. That said, you can avoid misunderstandings about this by making the school application and acceptance a prerequisite to hiring the applicant.

Central Georgia Technical College and Penn Foster follow the Bureau of Apprenticeship and Training standards and are registered with our state apprenticeship council office. They both also helped me design my construction apprenticeship program to reflect the related training instruction portion of the DOL's registered apprenticeship program requirements.

The three components to an apprenticeship program are education, paid employment, and credentials. The educational component is finding a trusted education partner who is accredited and can provide an educational curriculum that meets your company needs. The best part about this is that most schools are eager to partner with employers because it benefits both you and them. You get to train your employees, they increase their student population, and both of you can feed each other's pipelines for school and employment. It's a victory for both partners.

RELATED INSTRUCTION OUTLINE
Construction Worker/Laborer

O*NET-SOC CODE: _____ **RAPIDS CODE:** _____

Base Program: Candidates will attend school (RTI) and work (OJT), splitting days in half (4 hours each, all 8 hours paid).

Course Title	Number	Duration (hours)
Year One (185 hours)		
Trades Safety, Getting Started	186101	5
Career Readiness Orientation	588900	2.5
Jobs, Companies, and the Economy:		
Basic Concepts for Employees	186191	5
Addition and Subtraction	186303	5
Linear and Distance Measurement	186125	5
Multiplication and Division	186304	5
Materials Handling Safety	186109	10
Personal Skills—Integrity	588001	2.5

This excerpt from a course outline at Penn Foster gives an idea of the topics covered and time dedicated to each.

The following list of general and specialty tasks represent skills required by a Construction Craft Laborer (CCL) in a high performance industry. The skills required of a CCL are diverse and many. They work on buildings, highways and heavy construction sites; tunnel and shaft excavations; demolition and environmental remediation sites. CCLs may be removing asbestos or lead-based paint from buildings. CCLs also erect and disassemble scaffolding, they load and unload building materials, tend numerous machines and work with other trades including carpenters, plasters, operating engineers and masons. CCLs also clear and prepare highway work zones, install traffic barricades, markers, and control traffic. They install sewer, water and storm drain pipes and place concrete and asphalt on roads. Other highly specialized tasks include operating laser equipment to place pipes, operating air, electric and pneumatic tools. CCLs also operate a variety of equipment including pavement breakers jackhammers, earth tampers, concrete, mortar and plaster mixers, electric and hydraulic boring machines, torches, small mechanical hoists, laser beam equipment, and surveying and measuring equipment. In general, the skills represent competencies in managing and understanding resources, information, technology, systems, and interpersonal relations.

The following general skills should be mastered by all Construction Craft Laborers.

APPROXIMATE HOURS

I.	General Skills	1,600-2,100 hours
A.	Site/Project Preparation and Maintenance	600-800 hours
	• clearing, bucking, and falling	
	• transportation, dismantling, and stockpiling of scaffolding	
	• and work platforms	
	• grading and compaction	
	• layout and staking protocols	
	• rigging & signaling for work traditionally performed by CCLs	
	• site preparation, clean-up, and security	
B.	Tools, Equipment, and Materials	600-800 hours
	• tool, equipment, and material recognition and preparation	
	• hand electric, gas, diesel, pneumatic, and power tool	
	• equipment use and maintenance	
	• tool, equipment, and material storage and security	
C.	Safety	400-500 hours

This excerpt from the DOL site provides a look at what work hours categorized by apprenticeship skill could look like.

The second component, paid employment, means you must give apprenticeship participants relevant on-the-job training. At my company, we correlate our on-the-job training with the curriculum outlined by both schools. A subcomponent to this is that participants must have a mentor who provides one-on-one mentoring, meaning for each student, there must be a mentor assigned to them to ensure competency of skill and successful completion within the program. The best way to address this, in some instances, is to recruit another professional to help with the student's on-the-job learning or identify a union that may wish to be a part of the project and have your employees join the union with memberships. Furthermore, some unions may not have apprenticeship programs up and running, so they might be interested in helping their members connect with you for apprenticeship opportunities. Another option is going to your local career center and posting a job listing for licensed individuals. You cannot skimp on this program component, so think it through to ensure you can execute it properly. Having licensed individuals as mentors helps reinforce what the participants are learning in school and also adds credibility to your program by showing those same participants that they could be teachers someday and give back to newbies in the industry as licensed individuals themselves.

The last component, credentials, is a direct result of participants attending the related course instruction through your education partner. All participants who go through your registered apprenticeship program will receive at least one certification that is applicable to the industry; they can even use the credential outside of your particular program. It's up to you to coordinate these three components to your apprenticeship, and it's up to the participant to keep up on them all.

Even if they decide not to continue working for you through the whole apprenticeship, they can continue with the educational component. That's their prerogative, but it can cause strain on your program to have participants start and not continue their apprenticeship. I encourage you to keep that in mind when you interview your candidates to ensure they are committed to staying with your program. I also think it's important to let them know that if they drop out of school, they can jeopardize their future financial aid. Our company provides all this information during our pre-hiring information sessions so that participants understand the big picture of the apprenticeship program just as much as the company and the education partners do.

Central Georgia Technical College offers a clear definition of what a registered apprenticeship entails.

Penn Foster has an excellent listing of workforce development apprenticeship programs.

CHAPTER 8

Choose the Right Mentor

You must provide on-the-job training that reflects the students' course instruction from the school you are partnering with. Your company's one-the-job trainers will provide one-on-one support for apprentices, so choosing them is the most important component of this process. Much like the education portion, there is no program if you do not have competent mentors to help each student successfully complete your company's program. The mentors should be licensed or certified in their respective fields and have a deep understanding of the craft they are teaching. In addition, their availability must be flexible and consistent. Lastly, they must commit to the entire program period—remember, 4,000 hours is equivalent to two years. Mentoring is great for people in your industry who no longer wish to do hands-on work and manual labor.

According to an article in *Forbes*,[26] the eight qualities that make great leaders are enthusiasm, integrity, communication skills, loyalty, decisiveness, managerial competence, empowerment, and charisma. I must stress that your mentors' leadership skills are what will make your apprenticeship program succeed. Yes, all eight of these leadership qualities are essential. Let's take a closer look at why each one of them is so important.

---

26. https://www.forbes.com/sites/kimberlyfries/2018/02/08/8-essential-qualities-that-define-great-leadership/#4edf8b3f3b63

Enthusiasm

An individual with sincere enthusiasm will show pure authenticity and model for your participants their authenticity as a leader. There is nothing more exciting to me than watching people who love their job, display it openly. When a person has passion for their trade, it shows in how they execute their skills. In this same respect, these people will be competent and confident in their training approach for the employees in your program.

A mentor who is passionate about their work will also model a strong work ethic, are fun, show empathy, are energetic, are optimism, display work excellence, have focus, have drive, and are self-motivation. The measurement of this person's character can be seen in everything they do. I call this person—and their leadership qualities—a total package. People who love what they do are infectious; they inspire slackers to come to service. You want high-performing individuals, not mediocre, just-getting-by workers. Sincerely enthusiastic leaders are the start of creating this type of high-performing organization.

Integrity

Integrity is defined as the things that people do when others are not around. This quality will ultimately reflect in the organizational culture that is created for your company. What this means is that the tail is only as good as the head. Good leaders do what's right in the absence of authority and encourage your team to do the same. People with integrity do not take shortcuts; they have self-accountability and respect themselves and others. The leader who has integrity is trusted and encourages the same integrity in others.

Communication Skills

Communication begins and ends all transactions. If you cannot articulate yourself to others, how will they understand your perspective? How will they gauge how to respectfully interact with you? In a job setting, good leaders can clearly express their needs to an employer, and they are open to reciprocal interactions that may include constructive criticism. They are open to expressing themselves both verbally and in writing, and they are proficient at both—or at least wise enough to ask for help where they need it. They are cognizant of their nonverbal communication as well and use all three modes to interact positively with staff. Leaders with this quality are successful because they are malleable and flexible, and they show grace and ease when interacting with all levels of employees.

Loyalty

Loyal people see the long-term vision of an organization and are going to stay and see it through. They are dependable and respect the culture they agreed to be a part of, and they do not do so in a malicious way or in opposition to company policy or people. They know how to display their allegiance to the company in their daily behaviors.

Decisiveness

Leaders who can make decisions and execute company directives are the ideal people for conveying objectives from the owner and upper management to the workforce. A decisive leader can make decisions, be flexible in addressing challenges that may arise, and problem-solve easily. They can identify ways to positively fix company challenges. Their ability to identify decisions that can influence change is helpful and allows employers to trust them as dependable employees.

Empowerment

Good leaders can influence, motivate, and foster involvement from your participants because they have empowerment capabilities. They typically meet people where they are, help others sharpen their skills, give constructive criticism that leaves individual character intact, and push people to new heights while creating a high-performing culture. They hold themselves and others accountable through leading and following.

Charisma

Charismatic leaders are good to people, know how to show people that they are worthy of a good work environment, and are willing to help boost morale. They tend to be people magnets, so be mindful that people will want to be around them and follow them. In leadership, that's good, but it can be distracting at times because people will track their every move, even leading to stalled operations if that person is not present. Some charismatic leaders will help to no end, which can sometimes lead to stunting participants' ability to work and think on their own. A balanced leader, however, will both help participants and motivate them to learn and do well.

Managerial Competence

Wow! I have met a lot of people with managerial titles that lack the competencies that should go with those leadership positions. Managerial competence is a mastery of all the qualities described in this section combined with the ability to leverage them effectively. A person who possesses this skill knows how to demonstrate these qualities in a way that makes people want to follow what they do and say. They are "boss types" because they influence, lead, resolve conflict, model emotional intelligence, know how to build teams, think critically, influence change when needed, motivate, choose good-quality candidates, and manage their performance. These individuals are personable and trusted by employees. Leaders in managerial positions in your company need to have a firm grasp of these qualities in order to represent your business well.

Combined, all of these characteristics make for excellent leaders. Beyond that, though, these are qualities for people at any level to strive for because they foster a high-performing culture. Ideal apprenticeship mentors possess a combination of these qualities, see themselves as equal contributors, and work to be successful within the sum of the whole organization.

You've already got a plan to approach retired leaders in your industry (referral agencies). If you don't know them personally, ask around. The DOL website has many services to help you fulfill your program requirements. Use all of them, where applicable. Your focus will be on the "Employer" tab for resources, or you can use the search box. I discovered that a search for "industry and equity intermediaries" was very helpful to find my program mentors.

These search filters show results for apprenticeships near Macon, Georgia, listed on Apprenticeship.gov.

PART III

The Meat and Potatoes

CHAPTER 9

Apply to the Department of Labor Apprenticeship Program

Y ou've learned about apprenticeship programs and why they're a good idea for your business, and you've done the planning work to identify your vision, target audiences, education partners, and curriculum. Now you're ready to apply to the DOL Apprenticeship Program!

Before you begin, you need an account with login.gov, which is a secure portal for government programs. This will be what you sign in with for the Registered Apprenticeship Program. Click "Create an Account."

The account creation page displays where you will log in.

When you have your portal login, you can use that to begin the application process. You should know in advance that this process can take a while, and by the time you're reading this,

I pray that the website is up and fully functioning because at the time of writing (November 2019), it had some functionality issues. The user interface was not easy to navigate when I initially applied, and that caused me to lose everything I had entered into their system. I misunderstood what the application was asking me, and when it was submitted, it was fully blank. I then had to go back and retype it. However, it allowed for me to ask questions for clarity and do it correctly the next time around. While it took some time for this process to come to a close, I was able to form some valuable partnerships with the people who helped me during this time, and that changed the trajectory of my program.

While I hope you form valuable partnerships as well, I also hope it is not because of challenges with the application process! That changes your trajectory. Let's keep focus. To make it easier for you than it was for me, follow these steps:

1. Go to https://dol.appiancloud.com/suite/sites/registered-apprenticeship. This will be the first page you will see. Click "Agree."

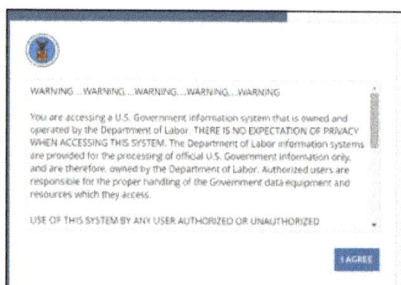

When you log in to the DOL site, you must first accept the terms in the disclaimer.

2. Next you should see this page requesting portal login credentials. Enter your information and click "Sign In."

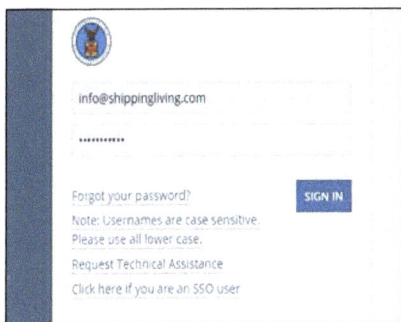

Continue logging in to the DOL site.

3. Once fully logged in, you will have entered the Standards Builder portal. You will be asked to fill in your profile, which reflects your company's information. When this book was written, I had already completed this portal, so mine looks different than your screen will, but it's similar. You should see a blue plus sign, and when you hover over it, it says, "Create a new apprenticeship program" if this is your first program. If you have one already and are adding a new program, it will say, "Create another apprenticeship program."

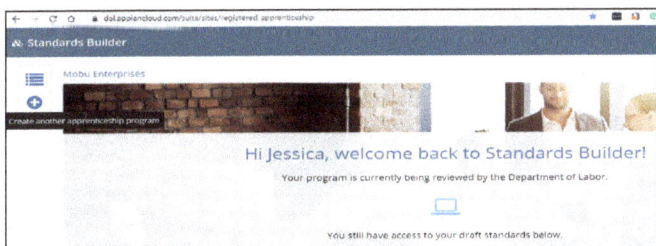

You'll first be taken to the Standards Builder portal.

4. Once you click on the plus sign, it should go to this page. Fill in the form and click "Next."

Let's start by getting to know you!

We just need a few details to get us rolling.

Sponsor Name *

enter the name of your organization

Address *

City *

State *

Choose a State

Zip Code *

County *

Choose a County

First Name *

Jessica

Last Name *

Lupo

Start by entering information about your business and yourself.

5. You will be given contact information for your assigned apprenticeship state director's information—your point of contact for your region. Save this information. Then click "Ok, Let's Get Started."

Nice to meet you, Jessica.

We look forward to helping you develop your apprenticeship program located in Georgia.

Meet your Apprenticeship State Director!

Your State Director is available to help you with the development of your program.

👤 La Verne Coleman
📞 (404) 302-5489
✉️ coleman_averne@dol.gov

The state director has been notified and is willing to answer any questions you have.

What's Next?

Next, select your occupation from the Department of Labor's list of apprenticeable occupations.

BACK   OK, LET'S GET STARTED

You will be assigned a DOL representative.

> Tip: Remember to click "Save" on every page so you do not lose your progress.

> Before proceeding, check your email to be sure you're receiving the necessary confirmations. You should receive two emails once you initially sign up. They would read like this:

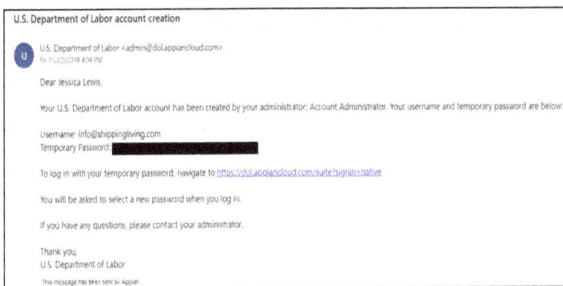

You will receive two emails confirming your Standards Builder account creation with username and password.

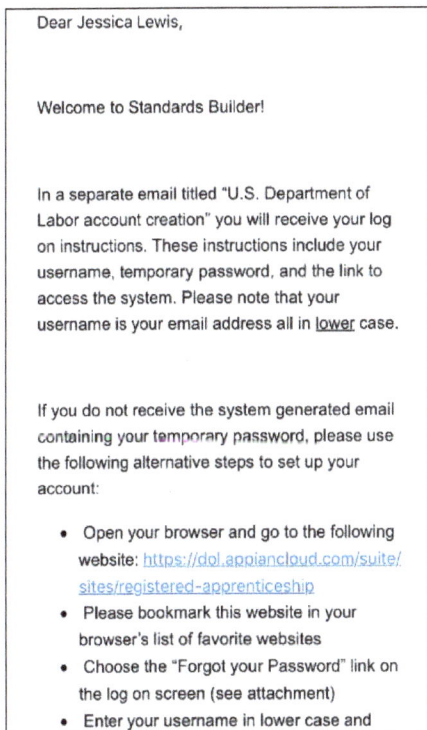

Dear Jessica Lewis,

Welcome to Standards Builder!

In a separate email titled "U.S. Department of Labor account creation" you will receive your log on instructions. These instructions include your username, temporary password, and the link to access the system. Please note that your username is your email address all in lower case.

If you do not receive the system generated email containing your temporary password, please use the following alternative steps to set up your account:

- Open your browser and go to the following website: https://dol.appiancloud.com/suite/sites/registered-apprenticeship
- Please bookmark this website in your browser's list of favorite websites
- Choose the "Forgot your Password" link on the log on screen (see attachment)
- Enter your username in lower case and

The second confirmation email provides instructions on how to access your account if you did not receive the first email.

6. You will then see this page, which lists all the require-
    ments of the Registered Apprenticeship Program.

    Note: Read this carefully. This is how you are being held
    accountable for being a rep.

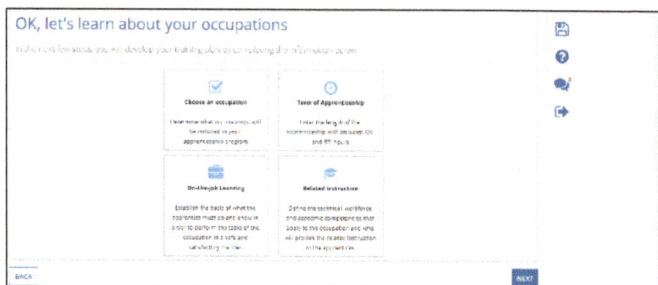

This screen provides a quick view of the program setup requirements and outline of expected objectives.

7. The next pages are where you get to choose your occu-
    pation for your apprenticeship program. You can choose
    from the ones listed, or if you do not see your occupation,
    do a search. Click "Add Occupation" when you find your
    choice. If your choice is not available, call your appren-
    ticeship state director.

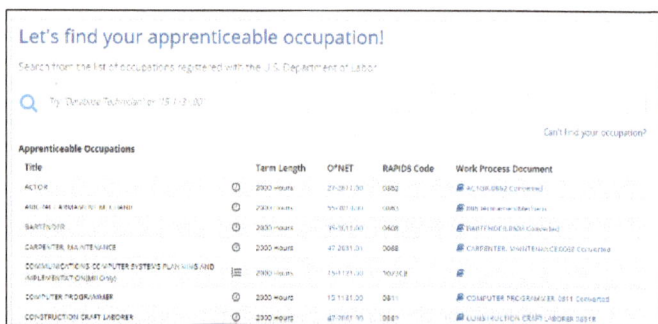

The search box helps you select the occupation your apprenticeship serves.

8. Notice there were 1,425 occupations when I did my search, and not all had a work process document (WPD). Work Process document summarizes the core competencies one must experience during an apprenticeship program. This means you may have to create your own, which can easily be done by working with your state director and education partner. Contact them both and explain that a WPD is not available for your occupation in the Registered Apprenticeship Program application. There are apprenticeships available for most types of jobs, so don't worry—that is why they are partnering with you. Resources are available to ensure you are successful. Be fearless and ask for help.

9. The next page should show the required hours and WPDs for your occupation. Confirm your choice by clicking "Next."

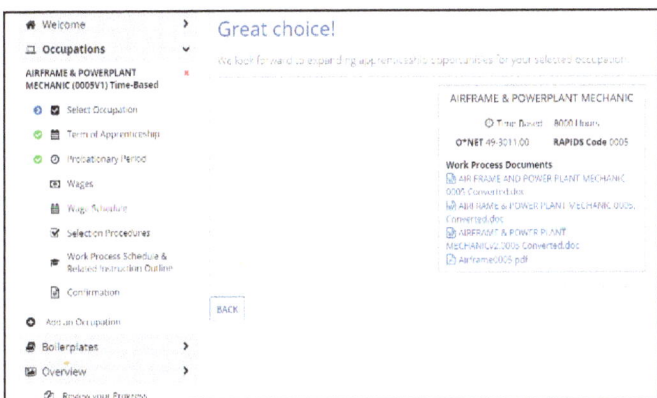

When you select an occupation, you will see a quick overview of the requirements for apprenticeships in that occupation.

Note: In the left sidebar, each step you've taken so far is marked with a green checkmark. This illustrates that the task has been successfully completed.

10. The next screen is about the term of the apprenticeship (minimally 4,000 hours), which includes the on-the-job training and related technical instruction. If your occupation has a WPD in the system, this is automatically filled in on your behalf. There is nothing to be added. If it's missing, then contact your state director. Click "Next."

Let's learn about your apprenticeship term

How long will your apprenticeship program take to complete?

What is the total length (in hours) of your apprenticeship program? *

8000

The term of an approved time-based occupation can be increased or decreased by 25%. The term of a time-based occupation cannot be less than 2000 hours.

Hours of related instruction (per year only) *

144

BACK   NEXT

The apprenticeship term, or number of hours, varies by occupation.

11. From there, we enter probationary period information. Just like the term, if your occupation has a WPD, this is automatically filled in on your behalf. There is nothing to be added. If it's missing, then contact your state director. Click "Next."

Let's add your probationary period

Every applicant selected for apprenticeship will serve a probationary period.

Total Length of Program
8000 Hours

How long (in hours) is the probationary period for apprentices? *

2000

The probationary period is typically calculated to be 25% of the length of the program, or 1 year, whichever is less.

? What is a probation period?

BACK   NEXT

Part of the apprenticeship term is spent in a probationary period.

12. Next is the wages screen. This page is asking for your graduation rate, meaning what your apprentices will earn upon graduation of your apprenticeship program. Wages are typically based on averages for your industry. You ultimately

choose what you want to pay your apprentice, but it must be commensurate to the industry. Mine is $30/hour.

Let's learn about your occupation's wages

This lets you enter the journeyworker wage

Journeyworker Wage (hourly)

$35.00

The probationary period is typically calculated to be 25% of the length of the program, or 1 year, whichever is less.

? What is a journeyworker?

BACK   NEXT

The wage entered in this window is the professional wage upon completion of the apprenticeship program.

13. The wage schedule screen records how your wages will progress over the course of the apprenticeship. Remember, progressive wages are a requirement. At Mobu, apprentice pay starts at $15/hour, and every six months and 1,200 hours, apprentices earn an additional $5/hour. By the end of our apprenticeship program they would have had four increases and end up at the $30/hour listed in the previous step. Progressive wages are a requirement. They will receive a final $10 raise and graduate at $40/hour upon becoming permanent employees.

Let's start entering your wage schedule

Registered Apprenticeship programs are required to guarantee a progressive wage.

Entry Wage	Completion Wage	Wage Rate
$15.00	$25.00	Hourly
The wage at which the apprentice will start.	The wage the apprentice will make at the end of the apprenticeship.	Choose the rate at which the apprentice will be paid.

? What if I want to add more detail to my wage schedule?

BACK   NEXT

In this screen, enter the progressive wage schedule, showing what your apprentices will be paid upon entering the program compared to upon completion.

14. Next, the system needs to know about your selection procedures. These include how your operation will recruit,

interview, make offers to, and accept apprentices into your program. These answers will be based on your policy and procedure manual and human resource (HR) hiring practices. If you do not already have something in place, hire a consultant or HR professional to help with this. There are plenty of templates online as well, which are standard for most HR processes.

The DOL monitors which selection procedures apprenticeship programs use to hire apprentices.

15. The second-to-last screen is about the work process schedule and related instruction outline. This is a document that describes how you will incorporate the on-the-job training with the apprenticeship program model requirements. Use the templates and add a description for how apprentices will be paired with a mentor/instructor to test learned knowledge competencies.

This screen gives a quick view of the work process schedule setup.

Also include an outline of the skills they will learn, including those that will be focused on during on-the-job training, and how many hours will be dedicated to each skill.

```
Short version
Related Instruction Descriptions
        Approximate Hours: 1,381

I. General Construction (866 hours)
Basic Safety (Construction Site Safety Orientation) (25 Hours)
Basic Communication Skills (15 Hours)
Basic Employability Skills (15 Hours)
Construction Math (20 Hours)
Introduction to Hand Tools (20 Hours)
Introduction to Power Tools (20 Hours)
Introduction to Construction Drawings (20 Hours)
Introduction to Basic Rigging (15 Hours)
Introduction to Material Handling (10 Hours)
Introduction to Masonry (25 Hours)
Masonry Units and Installation Techniques (120 Hours)
Floor Systems (55 Hours)
Ceiling Joist and Roof Framing (80 Hours)
Roofing Applications (50 Hours)
Wall Systems (40 Hours)
Exterior Finishing (70 Hours)
Basic Stair Layout (25 Hours)
Electrical Safety (20 Hours).
Residential Electrical Services (30 Hours)
Introduction to HVAC (15 Hours)
Introduction to Drain, Waste, and Vent (DWV) Systems (20 Hours)
Plastic Pipe and Fittings (25 Hours)
Copper Pipe and Fittings (25 Hours)
Cabinetmaking (70 Hours)
Cabinet Installation (20 Hours)
Modular Building construction (16 hours):

II. Masonry (245 hours)
Introduction to Masonry (25 Hours)
Masonry Safety (35 Hours)
```

Here's an excerpt from O*Net's outline and hours for each skill.

After uploading the document, click "Agree" to share your outline to other potential sponsors. This helps your peers, especially if you are the first one to add to an occupation. Then click "Next." You should also see a confirmation after uploading your work process document and schedule.

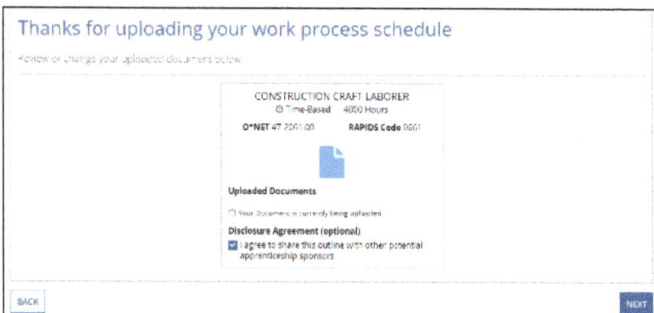

Thanks for uploading your work process schedule

Review or change your uploaded documents below

CONSTRUCTION CRAFT LABORER
Time-Based   4000 Hours

O*NET 47-2061.00   RAPIDS Code 0001

Uploaded Documents

Your Document is currently being uploaded

Disclosure Agreement (optional)
☑ I agree to share this outline with other potential apprenticeship sponsors

BACK   NEXT

When your upload is successful, you'll see this confirmation screen.

16. Finally, you will see the confirmation page.

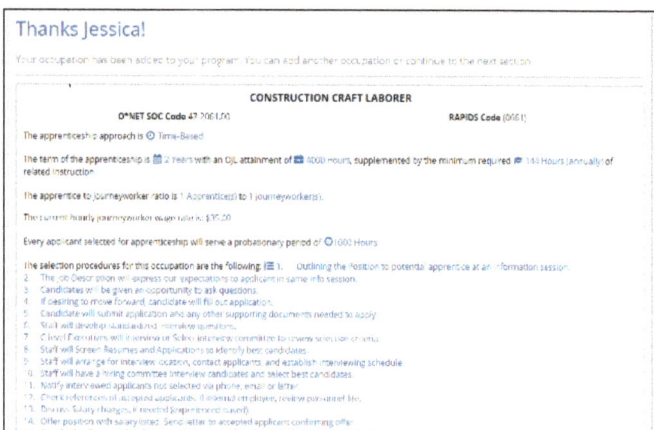

Thanks Jessica!

Your occupation has been added to your program. You can add another occupation or continue to the next section.

CONSTRUCTION CRAFT LABORER

O*NET SOC Code 47-2061.00   RAPIDS Code (0001)

The apprenticeship approach is Time-Based

The term of the apprenticeship is 2 Years with an OJL attainment of 4000 Hours, supplemented by the minimum required 144 Hours (Annually) of related instruction

The apprentice to journeyworker ratio is 1 Apprentice(s) to 1 Journeyworker(s).

The current hourly journeyworker wage rate is $15.00

Every applicant selected for apprenticeship will serve a probationary period of 1000 Hours

The selection procedures for this occupation are the following:
1. Outlining the Position to potential apprentice at an information session.
2. The Job Description will express our expectations to applicant in same info session.
3. Candidates will be given an opportunity to ask questions.
4. If desiring to move forward, candidate will fill out application.
5. Candidate will submit application and any other supporting documents needed to apply.
6. Staff will develop standardized interview questions.
7. Chosen Executives will interview or Select interviewer committee to screen selection criteria.
8. Staff will Screen Resumes and Applications to identify best candidates.
9. Staff will arrange for interview location, contact applicants and establish interviewing schedule.
10. Staff will have a hiring committee interview candidates and select best candidates.
11. Notify interviewed applicants not selected via phone, email or letter.
12. Once selection has been accepted applicants, if external employee, review personnel file.
13. Review Salary changes, if needed (experienced hires).
14. Offer position with salary listed. Send letter to accepted applicant confirming offer.

This personalized confirmation screen is record that your occupation and other details were added to your program.

Final Step: Boilerplate Standards

1. Choose the minimum qualifications necessary for an apprentice to start your program. Then click "Next." Need help? Contact your state director or another sponsor.

OK, let's deterimine your minimum qualifications

Driver's License
A valid drivers license is required.

Minimum Age
16
An apprentice must be at least 16 years of age, except where a higher age is required by law.

Educational Requirements

Physical Requirements
Drug Screen

Aptitude Tests

Other Qualifications

List all other requirements

BACK   NEXT

Next it's time to enter minimum qualifications for your apprenticeship program.

2. The next page asks you to choose whether or not your apprentices will be paid. Remember, if you choose not to pay them, your program cannot become a registered apprenticeship program with the DOL. Choose whether your program will be paid or unpaid, and then click "Next."

Let's find out more about your related training

Will apprentices be paid for hours spent attending related instruction classes?

Yes. Apprentices will be paid for hours spent attending related instruction classes.

No. Apprentices will not be paid for hours spent attending related instruction classes.

? What is related instruction?

BACK   NEXT

Whether or not you will pay your apprentices is a crucial question.

3. Will you give your participants credit for previous experience?

OK, now let's set up credit for previous experience

Apprentice applicants can seek credit for previous experience gained outside the supervision of the sponsor

Apprentice applicants seeking credit for previous experience gained outside the apprenticeship program must furnish such transcripts, records, affidavits, etc. that may be appropriate to substantiate the claim.

Enter any additional requirements for an apprentice to receive credit for previous experience

Additional Requirements

Participants can receive credit for past experience and must furnish such transcripts, records, affidavits, etc.

BACK   NEXT

Many apprentices appreciate receiving credit for previous experience

4. Equal Employment Opportunity acceptance page. Read this in full, and then click "Next."

OK, now for your Equal Opportunity Pledge

Equal Employment Opportunity pledges can be updated to apply in additional protected bases

Equal Opportunity Pledge
Mobu Enterprises will not discriminate against apprenticeship applicants or apprentices based on race, color, religion, national origin, sex (including pregnancy and gender identity), sexual orientation, genetic information, or because they are an individual with a disability or a person 40-years old or older.

Enter any additional protected bases (as applicable per the sponsor's state or locality):

Additional Protected Bases

The next screen is the Equal Opportunity Pledge, where you agree to not discriminate.

Woo-hoo! Congratulations; you've now completed the portion of your application that requires documentation.

CHAPTER 10

Play the Waiting Game

Now that you've completed your application, it's time to await a confirmation email from the DOL that shows your submission was accepted.

U.S. Department of Labor account creation

U.S. Department of Labor <admin@dol.appiancloud.com>
Fri 11/25/2019 3:04 PM

Dear Jessica Lewis,

Your U.S. Department of Labor account has been created by your administrator: Account Administrator. Your username and temporary password are below:

Username: info@shippingliving.com
Temporary Password:

To log in with your temporary password, navigate to https://dol.appiancloud.com/suite?signin=native

You will be asked to select a new password when you log in.

If you have any questions, please contact your administrator.

Thank you,
U.S. Department of Labor
This message has been sent by Appian

The DOL will email you a confirmation that you have created your account.

CHAPTER 11

Meet Your Department of Labor Representative

A DOL rep will reach out to you and schedule a time to discuss your program in detail and ask you any questions needed for clarity. This conversation is to ensure you understand the requirements for running a registered apprenticeship program and that you agree to follow them. Otherwise, if you proceed but have misunderstood the legalities of running an apprenticeship program, you could lose your Registered Apprenticeship Program title, along with all the benefits that come with it.

Good Afternoon Jessica,

How are you? I am the Apprenticeship and Training Representative assisting the State Director in the development of your program. Are you available to teleconference on the following dates and/or times:

· **Monday, February 3, 2020 at 1:30 PM** OR
· **Tuesday, February 4, 2020 at 10:30 AM**

Once the teleconference is confirmed then I will send the dialing instructions. Look forward to speaking with you soon. Thank you for your support of Registered Apprenticeship!

The initial teleconference request by your assigned DOL representative will look like this.

CHAPTER 12

Receive Final Approval

O nce this conversation takes place, the DOL will take time to review your submission and give you the final approval. Once approved, you can use your registered apprenticeship program to your company's advantage. Read the next chapter to see how.

Good Afternoon Jessica,

Congratulations! The Mobu Enterprises Standards of Apprenticeship have been approved. Attached are the new sponsor user guides for the RAPIDS System and a copy of the approved Standards of Apprenticeship. You will receive a separate e-mail with instructions on to access the RAPIDS System. If you have any questions, please notify me for assistance. Thank you for your support of Registered Apprenticeship!

When you receive this email, congratulations—your program has been accepted!

Jessica Lewis,

You have been added to program number **2020-GA-78754** by █████████████.

You can access RAPIDS 2.0 at the following URL:

https://dol.appiancloud.com/suite

Thank you

Finally, you will receive an email like this confirming your company has been added to the DOL database and instructions on accessing the system as a registered apprenticeship program

PART IV

The Dessert

CHAPTER 13

What's Next for Your Program

Since registering and launching Mobu's apprenticeship program, I have seen excellent benefits. For one, my partner and I are social entrepreneurs, and this program is helping us and the local jurisdictions we serve in the following ways. Maybe one of these will resonate with you:

- We are creating a customized skilled labor force. We know the competencies and weaknesses of each individual we hire and train, we support them through proper training and one-on-one mentorship, and we can be better leaders and managers, all of which helps their success.
- We are supporting the local economy by providing services to local residents and businesses.
- We are encouraging the use of education as a tool to heighten and strengthen skill sets. Using local schools and encouraging advanced education helps broaden people's mindsets by exposing them to new opportunities.
- We are helping our community by building sustainable houses. These houses are green, waterproof, fireproof, and windproof. They last longer than standard homes and are nontoxic, allowing the people who live in them to have better health overall.
- We are aiding in the self-esteem and positive mentality of our apprentices. By hiring people and giving them

a chance, we are fostering confidence and encouraging positive interactions and loyalty among the team.

- We are improving our participants' lifestyles by paying higher wages than other positions that may be available to them.

- We are creating new job opportunities. This is especially important in locales where good jobs are scarce, poverty is prevalent, and crime is high. Apprenticeship programs give people and communities hope for the future.

Of course we love that our program supports the community. It also supports us. Here are the business benefits:

- Registering our apprenticeship program has opened doors for grant and federal money through workforce development programs in our state. The WIOA is just one of these programs, and there are many others that are specific to different groups of people (such as ex-offenders, veterans, and youth).

- Registering our apprenticeship program has given our business additional credibility.

- Our community has grown through the many kind and helpful people who have assisted us in setting up our apprenticeship program.

- Because I created the curriculum for our apprenticeship program, I can incorporate elements from my entrepreneur schooling, leadership curriculum, and other classes as an added value to our participants that enhances their soft skills. This in turn benefits the culture of the workplace.

This is a short ebook, but it's filled with all the steps you need to register your apprenticeship program. As you've learned, you do not have to be registered with the DOL to do an apprenticeship program, but the benefits to your community and your business are vast if you do.

Thank you for reading. If you would like assistance in any of these steps, please email me at info@shippingliving.com for a consultation.

Further Resources

Department of Labor Apprenticeship website: This website is run by the DOL and has a host of information for employers, apprentices, and educators. www.apprenticeship.gov

Department of Labor Employment and Training Administration Technical Assistance: This webpage lists help desk email addresses. Don't hesitate to reach out for help during your application process. www.doleta.gov/Performance/technicalassistance/eta_default.cfm

Photographer: Bart Law

Jessica Lewis was born and raised in Philadelphia, Pennsylvania, and currently resides in Macon, Georgia. During her time in Philadelphia, she started a business consultancy firm named Real Solutions for Real People. Her motto is "We help real people find solutions to their everyday problems personally and professionally." She also hosted a radio show named *All about Beauty, Business*, which focused on the beauty industry, entrepreneurs, and community-related current events.

Jessica holds a bachelor of science in psychology from Pennsylvania State University and a master of business management from Colorado Technical University, which gives her the people and business skills necessary to help entrepreneurs like herself get their businesses up, running, and thriving. As a result of her business education and over eighteen years of entrepreneurial experience, she came up with the *Entrepreneur Spotlight* television show, which highlights entrepreneurs and the great products or services they provide. The show's Q&A portion showcases the personality, character, and professionalism of each guest. Aside from *Entrepreneur Spotlight*, Jessica has also aired several podcasts relating to personal and business credit, finance, and asset protection. Her greatest accomplishment so far is spreading her knowledge about business to the masses via her various entertainment platforms.

With over fifteen years of experience working in almost every capacity of human services, Jessica has a keen insight into human behaviour. As a result, she started the business finance division of Real Solutions for Real People, through which she helps business owners (both for-profit and nonprofit) procure financing to help them expand their organizations. Being a forward thinker has also allowed her to start Mobu Enterprises, a green construction firm that builds residential and commercial structures out of shipping containers. In all her business ventures, Jessica's goal is to help people reach their dreams through education and action. The finance division allows her to help businesses tap into the credit game, and with the construction firm she helps people build their dream homes or commercial spaces. She believes "the sky is *not* the limit."

In Jessica's spare time, she plays with her dog, visits new eateries, and enjoys traveling. She volunteers with SCORE, Mini Hoops Basketball Camp, Macon Re-Entry Coalition, the Georgia Department of Juvenile Justice task force for recidivism reduction, Northeast High School, and the Young

Entrepreneurs Academy. Her other professional accomplishments include public speaking, hosting webinars, and launching massive successful marketing campaigns. Her main goal in life is to help everyone she encounters to reach their full potential. Upcoming projects include developing a tiny-home community, domestic and international affordable housing, commercial entertainment space, and coworking incubators. She is also seeking joint ventures on other business endeavours that will minimize crime and violence, eradicate self-hate among domestic violence and familial abuse victims, and reduce recidivism and homelessness in youth, veteran, and ex-offender communities. Learn more about Jessica at www.jessicamlewis.com.